KAPLAN

Other Kaplan Books for College-Bound Students

College Admissions and Financial Aid

Conquer the Cost of College

Parent's Guide to College Admissions

Scholarships

The Unofficial, ~~Un~~biased Insider's Guide to the 320 Most Interesting Colleges

The *Yale Daily News* Guide to Succeeding in College

Test Preparation

SAT Verbal Velocity

SAT Math Mania

SAT & PSAT

SAT Verbal Workbook

SAT Math Workbook

SAT Vocabulary Flashcards Flip-O-Matic

By the Staff of Kaplan, Inc.

Simon & Schuster

NEW YORK · LONDON · SINGAPORE · SYDNEY · TORONTO

Kaplan Publishing
Published by Simon & Schuster
1230 Avenue of the Americas
New York, NY 10020

Contributing Editors: Trent Anderson, Seppy Basili, Dan McGrew, and Justin Serrano

Project Editor: Megan Duffy

Cover Design: Cheung Tai

Production Manager: Michael Shevlin

Editorial Coordinator: Déa Alessandro

Executive Editor: Del Franz

November 2002
10 9 8 7 6 5 4 3 2 1
Manufactured in the United States of America
Published simultaneously in Canada

ISBN 0-7432-3522-3

HOW TO USE THIS BOOK

Kaplan's fantastic *SAT Vocabulary Flashcards Flip-O-Matic* is perfectly designed to help you learn 500 essential SAT vocabulary words in a quick, easy, and fun way. Simply read the vocabulary word on the front of the flashcard and then flip to the back to see its definition and an example sentence with the SAT word in action. Once you've mastered a particular word, clip or fold back the corner of the flashcard so that you can zip right by it on your next pass through the book. The *Flip-O-Matic* is packed with vocabulary—remember to flip the book over and flip through the other half!

As a special bonus, we've included an SAT word root list at the back of this book for extra studying power. Grouping words together that share a common root meaning is a terrific and efficient way to familiarize yourself with strange or tough words you may encounter on the test.

Looking for still more SAT prep? Be sure to pick up a copy of Kaplan's comprehensive *SAT & PSAT* guide, complete with full-length practice tests, or our *SAT Verbal Workbook* and *SAT Math Workbook*.

Good luck, and happy flipping!

someone passionately devoted to a cause

The religious *zealot* had no time for those who failed to share his strongly held beliefs.

ABASE

to humble; disgrace

After his immature behavior, John was *abased* in my eyes.

ZEALOT

to join together

As soon as the farmer had *yoked* his oxen together, he began to plow the fields.

ABDICATE

to give up a position, right, or power

With the angry mob clamoring outside the palace, the king *abdicated* his throne and fled.

YOKE (v.)

fear or hatred of foreigners or strangers

Countries in which *xenophobia* is prevalent often have more restrictive immigration policies than countries which are more accepting of foreign influences.

ABERRATION

something different from the usual

Due to the bizarre *aberrations* in the author's behavior, her publicist decided that the less the public saw of her, the better.

XENOPHOBIA

withered, shriveled, wrinkled

The *wizened* old man was told that the plastic surgery necessary to make him look young again would cost more money than he could imagine.

ABEYANCE

temporary suppression or suspension

Michelle held her excitement in *abeyance* while the college review board considered her application.

playful or fanciful idea

The ballet was *whimsical*, delighting the children with its imaginative characters and unpredictable sets.

ABJECT

miserable, pitiful

When we found the *abject* creature lying on the ground, we took it inside and tended to its broken leg.

WHIMSICAL

to sharpen, stimulate

The delicious odors wafting from the kitchen *whet* Jack's appetite, and he couldn't wait to eat.

ABSTRUSE

difficult to comprehend

The philosopher's elucidation was so clear that he turned an *abstruse* subject into one his audience could grasp.

burning, caustic; sharp, bitter

Given the opportunity to critique his enemy's new book, the spiteful critic wrote an unusually *vitriolic* review of it for the *New York Times*.

ACERBIC

bitter, sharp in taste or temper

Gina's *acerbic* wit and sarcasm were feared around the office.

VITRIOLIC

someone with masterly skill; expert musician

He is a *virtuoso* conductor and has performed in all the most prestigious concert halls.

ACQUIESCE

to agree; comply quietly

The princess *acquiesced* to demands that she marry a nobleman, but she was not happy about it.

VIRTUOSO

change or variation; ups and downs

Investors must be prepared for *vicissitudes* in the market and not panic when stock prices fall occasionally.

ACRIMONY

bitterness, animosity

The *acrimony* the newly divorced couple showed towards each other made everyone feel uncomfortable.

VICISSITUDE

trace, remnant

Vestiges of the former tenant still remained in the apartment, although he hadn't lived there for years.

ADULTERATE

to corrupt or make impure

The restaurateur made his ketchup last longer by *adulterating* it with water.

VESTIGE

quality of appearing true or real

The TV show's *verisimilitude* led viewers to believe that the characters it portrayed were real.

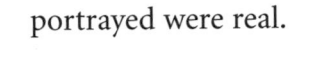

AESTHETIC

pertaining to beauty or art

The museum curator, with her fine *aesthetic* sense, created an exhibit that was a joy to behold.

VERISIMILITUDE

green with vegetation; inexperienced

He wandered deep into the *verdant* woods in search of mushrooms and other edible flora.

AGGRANDIZE

to make larger or greater in power

All the millionaire really wanted was to *aggrandize* his personal wealth as much as possible.

VERDANT

adore, honor, respect

In traditional Confucian society, the young *venerate* the older members of their village, and defer to the elders' wisdom.

ALACRITY

cheerful willingness, eagerness; speed

The eager dog fetched with *alacrity* the stick that had been tossed for him.

VENERATE

boasted about, bragged about

The much-*vaunted* new computer program turned out to have so many bugs that it had to be recalled.

ALLEGORY

symbolic representation

The novelist used the stormy ocean as an *allegory* for her life's struggles.

VAUNTED

tasteless, dull

Todd found his blind date *vapid* and boring, and couldn't wait to get away from her.

AMALGAMATE

to mix, combine

Giant Industries *amalgamated* with Mega Products to form Giant-Mega Products Incorporated.

VAPID

empty, void; lacking intelligence, purposeless

The congresswoman's *vacuous* speech angered the voters, who were tired of hearing empty platitudes.

AMELIORATE

to make better, improve

Conditions in the hospital were *ameliorated* by the hiring of dozens of expertly trained nurses.

VACUOUS

to waver, show indecision

The customer held up the line as he *vacillated* between ordering chocolate or coffee ice cream.

AMORTIZE

to diminish by installment payments

She was able to *amortize* her debts by paying a small amount each month.

VACILLATE

efficient, functional, useful

The suitcase was undeniably *utilitarian*, with its convenient compartments of different sizes, but it was also ugly.

ANACHRONISM

something chronologically inappropriate

The aged hippie used *anachronisms* like “groovy” and “far out” that had not been popular for years.

UTILITARIAN

to seize by force

The vice-principal was power-hungry, and threatened to *usurp* the principal's power.

ANATHEMA

ban, curse; something shunned or disliked

Sweaty, soiled clothing was *anathema* to the elegant Madeleine.

USURP

ANCILLARY

courteous, refined, suave

The *urbane* teenager sneered at the mannerisms of his country-bumpkin cousin.

accessory; subordinate; helping

Reforms were instituted at the main factory, but not at its *ancillary* plants, so defects continued to occur.

URBANE

to scold sharply

The teacher *upbraided* the student for scrawling graffiti all over the walls of the school.

ANTEDILUVIAN

prehistoric, ancient beyond measure

The *antediluvian* fossils were displayed in the museum.

UPBRAID

greasy, oily; smug and falsely earnest

The *unctuous* salesman showered the rich customers with exaggerated compliments.

ANTERIOR

preceding, previous, before, prior (to)

Following tradition, the couple's wedding was *anterior* to the honeymoon.

UNCTUOUS

ANTIPATHY

offense, resentment

The businessman took *umbrage* at the security guard's accusation that he had shoplifted a packet of gum.

dislike, hostility; extreme opposition or aversion

The *antipathy* between the French and the English regularly erupted into open warfare.

UMBRAGE

being everywhere simultaneously

Burger King franchises are *ubiquitous* in the United States, and are common in foreign countries as well.

APOCRYPHAL

not genuine; fictional

Sharon suspected that the stories she was hearing about alligators in the sewer were *apocryphal.*

UBIQUITOUS

beginner, novice

An obvious *tyro* at salsa, Millicent received no invitations to dance.

APOTHEOSIS

glorification; glorified ideal

In her heyday, many people considered Jackie Kennedy to be the *apotheosis* of stylishness.

TYRO

inherent vileness, foulness, depravity

The priest's affair with the teenage parishioner was considered an act of utter *turpitude.*

APPROBATION

praise; official approval

Billy was sure he had gained the *approbation* of his teacher when he received a glowing report card.

TURPITUDE

ARDENT

to cut off, shorten by cutting

The mayor *truncated* his standard lengthy speech when he realized that the audience was not in the mood to listen to it.

passionate, enthusiastic, fervent

After a 25-game losing streak, even the Mets' most *ardent* fans realized the team wouldn't finish first.

TRUNCATE

shallow, superficial

Lindsay's graduation speech was the same *trite* nonsense we've heard hundreds of times in the past.

ARDOR

great emotion or passion

Bishop's *ardor* for landscape was evident when he passionately described the beauty of the Hudson Valley.

TRITE

of slight worth, trivial, insignificant

That little glitch in the computer program is a *trifling* error; in general, it works really well.

ARDUOUS

extremely difficult, laborious

Amy thought she would pass out after completing the *arduous* climb up the mountain.

TRIFLING

fear and anxiety

Mike approached the door of the principal's office with *trepidation*.

ASCETIC

self-denying, abstinent, austere

The monk lived an *ascetic* life deep in the wilderness, denying himself all forms of luxury.

TREPIDATION

acute, sharp, incisive; forceful, effective

Dan's *trenchant* observations in class made him the professor's favorite student.

ASPERSION

false rumor, damaging report, slander

It is unfair to cast *aspersions* on someone behind his or her back.

TRENCHANT

obedient, yielding

Though it was exhausted, the *tractable* workhorse obediently dragged the carriage through the mud.

ASSIDUOUS

diligent, persistent, hard-working

The chauffeur scrubbed the limousine *assiduously*, hoping to make a good impression on his employer.

TRACTABLE

ASSUAGE

lethargic; unable to move; dormant

After surgery, the patient was *torpid* until the anesthesia wore off.

to make less severe, ease, relieve

Like many people, Philip Larkin used alcohol to *assuage* his sense of meaninglessness and despair.

TORPID

book, usually large and academic

The teacher was forced to refer to various *tomes* to find the answer to the advanced student's question.

ASTRINGENT

harsh, severe, stern

The principal's punishments seemed overly *astringent*, but the students did not dare to complain.

TOME

timid, shy, full of apprehension

A *timorous* woman, Lois relied on her children to act for her whenever aggressive behavior was called for.

ATROCIOUS

monstrous, shockingly bad, wicked

The British officer committed the *atrocious* act of slaughtering a large group of peaceful Indian villagers.

TIMOROUS

defensible, reasonable

Greg burned down his own house so that his ex-wife could not live in it, a scarcely *tenable* action in light of the fact that this also left his children homeless.

ATROPHY

to waste away, wither from disuse

When Mimi stopped exercising, her muscles began to *atrophy*.

TENABLE

digressing, diverting

Your argument is interesting, but it's *tangential* to the matter at hand, so I suggest we get back to the point.

ATTENUATE

to make thin or slender; weaken

The Bill of Rights *attenuated* the traditional power of government to change laws at will.

TANGENTIAL

silently understood or implied

Although not a word had been said, everyone in the room knew that a *tacit* agreement had been made about which course of action to take.

AUGURY

prophecy, prediction of events

Troy hoped the rainbow was an *augury* of good things to come.

TACIT

self-serving flatterer, yes-man

Dreading criticism, the actor surrounded himself with admirers and *sycophants*.

AUGUST

dignified, awe inspiring, venerable

The *august* view of the summit of the Grand Teton filled the climbers with awe.

SYCOPHANT

characterized by secrecy

The queen knew nothing of the *surreptitious* plots being hatched against her at court.

AUSPICIOUS

having favorable prospects, promising

Tamika thought that having lunch with the boss was an *auspicious* start to her new job.

SURREPTITIOUS

excessive amount

Because of the *surfeit* of pigs, pork prices have never been lower.

AVARICE

greed

Rebecca's *avarice* motivated her to stuff the $100 bill in her pocket instead of returning it to the man who had dropped it.

SURFEIT

arrogant, haughty, overbearing, condescending

She was a shallow and scornful society woman with a *supercilious* manner.

AXIOM

premise, postulate, self-evident truth

Halle lived her life based on the *axioms* her grandmother had passed on to her.

SUPERCILIOUS

too old, obsolete, outdated

The manual typewriter has become *superannuated*, although a few loyal diehards still swear by it.

BALEFUL

harmful, with evil intentions

The sullen teenager gave his nagging mother a *baleful* look.

SUPERANNUATED

trick or tactic used to avoid something

Spies who are not skilled in the art of *subterfuge* are generally exposed before too long.

BANAL

trite, overly common

He used *banal* phrases like "Have a nice day" or "Another day, another dollar."

SUBTERFUGE

to conquer, subdue; enslave

The Romans made a practice of *subjugating* all the peoples they conquered, often enslaving them.

BASTION

fortification, stronghold

The club was well known as a *bastion* of conservative values in the liberal city.

SUBJUGATE

to impair or reduce to uselessness

The company's leadership was *stultified* by its practice of promoting the owner's dimwitted children to powerful positions.

BELABOR

to insist repeatedly or harp on

I understand completely; you do not need to *belabor* the point.

STULTIFY

having or showing little emotion

The prisoner appeared *stolid* and unaffected by the judge's harsh sentence.

BELEAGUER

to harass, plague

Mickey's *beleaguered* parents finally gave in to his request for a Nintendo.

STOLID

indifferent to or unaffected by emotions

While most of the mourners wept, the dead woman's husband kept up a *stoic*, unemotional facade.

BELIE

to misrepresent; expose as false

The first lady's carefree appearance *belied* rumors that she was on the verge of divorcing her husband.

STOIC

self-restrained to the point of dullness

The lively young girl felt bored in the company of her *staid*, conservative date.

BELLICOSE

warlike, aggressive

Immediately after defeating one of his enemies, the *bellicose* chieftain declared war on another.

STAID

lacking authenticity; counterfeit, false

Quoting from a *spurious* bible, the cult leader declared that all property should be signed over to him.

BELLIGERENT

hostile, tending to fight

The bartender realized that it would be fruitless to try to subdue the *belligerent* drunk by himself.

SPURIOUS

sleepy or tending to cause sleep

The movie proved to be so *soporific* that soon loud snores were heard throughout the theater.

BENIGHTED

unenlightened

Ben scoffed at the crowd, as he believed it consisted entirely of *benighted* individuals.

SOPORIFIC

deceptive reasoning or argumentation

The politician used *sophistry* to cloud the issue whenever he was asked a tough question in a debate.

BEQUEATH

to give or leave through a will; to hand down

Grandpa *bequeathed* the house to his daughter and the car to his son.

SOPHISTRY

producing a full, rich sound

The *sonorous* blaring of the foghorn woke up Lily at 4:30 in the morning.

BESEECH

to beg, plead, implore

She *beseeched* him to give her a second chance, but he refused.

SONOROUS

drowsy, sleepy; inducing sleep

Carter became *somnolent* after taking a couple of sleeping pills.

BILK

to cheat, defraud

Though the lawyer seemed honest, the woman feared he would try to *bilk* her out of her money.

SOMNOLENT

belief that oneself is the only reality

Arthur's *solipsism* annoyed others, since he treated them as if they didn't exist.

BLANDISH

to coax with flattery

We *blandished* the bouncer with compliments until he finally let us into the club.

SOLIPSISM

grammatical mistake

The applicant's letter was filled with embarrassing *solecisms*, such as "I works here at 20 years."

BLIGHT (v.)

to afflict, destroy

The farmers feared that the previous night's frost had *blighted* the potato crops entirely.

SOLECISM

winding; intricate, complex

Thick, *sinuous* vines wound around the trunk of the tree.

BONHOMIE

good-natured geniality; atmosphere of good cheer

The general *bonhomie* that characterized the party made it a joy to attend.

SINUOUS

to smirk, smile foolishly

The spoiled girl *simpered* as her mother praised her extravagantly to the guests at the party.

BOON

blessing, something to be thankful for

Dirk realized that his new coworker's computer skills would be a real *boon* to the company.

SIMPER

angelic, pure, sublime

Selena's sweet, *seraphic* appearance belied her nasty, bitter personality.

BOURGEOIS

middle class

The *bourgeois* family was horrified when the lower-class family moved in next door.

SERAPHIC

aware, conscious, able to perceive

The anaesthetic didn't work and I was still *sentient* when the surgeon made her cut, so the operation was agony for me.

BREACH

act of breaking, violation

The record company sued the singer for *breach* of contract when he recorded for another company without permission.

SENTIENT

having a moralizing tone

The pastor took on a *sentientious* tone when he lectured the teenage couple on their loose morals.

BRIGAND

bandit, outlaw

Brigands held up the bank and made off with the contents of the safe.

SENTENTIOUS

aging, growing old

Fearful of becoming *senescent*, Jobim worked out several times a week and ate only health foods.

BRUSQUE

rough and abrupt in manner

The bank teller's *brusque* treatment of his customers soon evoked several complaints.

SENESCENT

narrow-minded; relating to a group or sect

Since the fall of Communism in the former Yugoslavia, its various ethnic groups have plunged into *sectarian* violence.

BURGEON

to sprout or flourish

We will need major subway expansion to accommodate the *burgeoning* population of the city.

SECTARIAN

vulgar, low, indecent

The decadent aristocrat took part in *scurrilous* activities every night, unbeknownst to his family.

BUTTRESS (v.)

to reinforce or support

The construction workers attempted to *buttress* the ceiling with pillars.

SCURRILOUS

CADENCE

to sparkle, flash

The society hostess was famous for her great wit and *scintillating* conversation.

rhythmic flow of poetry; marching beat

Pierre spoke with a lovely *cadence*, charming all those who heard him.

SCINTILLATE

trace amount

This poison is so powerful that no more of a *scintilla* of it is needed to kill a horse.

CAJOLE

to flatter, coax, persuade

The spoiled girl could *cajole* her father into buying her anything.

SCINTILLA

cynical, scornfully mocking

Denise was offended by the *sardonic* way in which her date made fun of her ideas and opinions.

CALLOW

immature, lacking sophistication

The young and *callow* fans hung on every word the talk show host said.

SARDONIC

CAPACIOUS

ruddy; cheerfully optimistic

A *sanguine* person thinks the glass is half full, while a depressed person thinks it's half empty.

large, roomy; extensive

We wondered how many hundreds of stores occupied the *capacious* mall.

SANGUINE

CAPITULATE

healthful

Rundown and sickly, Rita hoped that the fresh mountain air would have a *salubrious* effect on her health.

to submit completely, surrender

After atom bombs devastated Hiroshima and Nagasaki, the Japanese had little choice but to *capitulate*.

SALUBRIOUS

shrewd

Owls have a reputation for being *sagacious*, perhaps because of their big eyes which resemble glasses.

CAPRICIOUS

impulsive, whimsical, without much thought

> Queen Elizabeth I was quite *capricious*; her courtiers could never be sure who would catch her fancy.

SAGACIOUS

extremely sacred; beyond criticism

Many people considered Mother Teresa to be *sacrosanct* and would not tolerate any criticism of her.

CASTIGATE

to punish, chastise, criticize severely

Authorities in Singapore harshly *castigate* perpetrators of what would be considered minor crimes in the United States.

SACROSANCT

to contemplate, reflect upon

The scholars spent days at the retreat, *ruminating* upon the complexities of the geopolitical situation.

CATHARSIS

purification, cleansing

Plays can be more satisfying if they end in some sort of emotional *catharsis* for the characters involved.

RUMINATE

to make many holes in; permeate

The helicopter was *riddled* with bullet holes after its flight into the combat zone.

CATHOLIC

universal; broad and comprehensive

Hot tea with honey is a *catholic* remedy for a sore throat.

RIDDLE (v.)

humorous in a vulgar way

The court jester's *ribald* brand of humor delighted the rather uncouth king.

CAVALIER

carefree, happy; with lordly disdain

The nobleman's *cavalier* attitude towards the suffering of the peasants made them hate him.

RIBALD

boisterous festivity

An atmosphere of *revelry* filled the school after its basketball team's surprising victory.

CENTRIPETAL

directed or moving towards the center

It is *centripetal* force that keeps trains from derailing as they round curves.

REVELRY

to regroup, reorganize

After their humiliating defeat, the troops *retrenched* back at the base to decide what to do next.

CHAGRIN

shame, embarrassment, humiliation

> No doubt, the president felt a good deal of *chagrin* after vomiting on his neighbor at the state banquet.

RETRENCH

shy, modest, reserved

A shy and *retiring* man, Chuck was horrified at the idea of having to speak in public.

CHARLATAN

quack, fake

"That *charlatan* of a doctor prescribed the wrong medicine for me!" complained the patient.

RETIRING

group of attendants with an important person

The nobleman had to make room in his mansion not only for the princess, but also for her entire *retinue.*

CHICANERY

trickery, fraud, deception

Dishonest used car salesmen often use *chicanery* to sell their beat-up old cars.

RETINUE

not speaking freely; reserved

Physically small and *reticent*, Joan Didion often went unnoticed by those upon whom she was reporting.

CHOLERIC

easily angered, short-tempered

The *choleric* principal raged at the students who had come late to school.

RETICENT

impatient, uneasy, restless

The passengers became *restive* after having to wait in line for hours, and began to shout complaints at the airline staff.

CIRCUMLOCUTION

roundabout, lengthy way of saying something

He avoided discussing the real issues with endless *circumlocutions*.

RESTIVE

to reject as having no authority

The old woman's claim that she was Russian royalty was *repudiated* when DNA tests showed she was not related to them.

CIRCUMSCRIBE

to encircle; set limits on, confine

Diego Buenaventura's country estate is *circumscribed* by rolling hills.

REPUDIATE

morally unprincipled person

If you ignore your society's accepted moral code, you will be considered a *reprobate*.

CIRCUMSPECT

cautious, wary

His failures have made Jack far more *circumspect* in his exploits than he used to be.

REPROBATE

capable of being corrected

In the belief that the juvenile delinquent was *remediable* and not a hardened criminal, the judge put him on probation.

CLANDESTINE

secretive, concealed for a darker purpose

> The double agent paid many *clandestine* visits to the president's office in the dead of night.

REMEDIABLE

response

Patrick tried desperately to think of a clever *rejoinder* to Marcy's joke, but he couldn't.

CLEMENCY

merciful leniency

Kyle begged for *clemency*, explaining that he had been under the influence of hallucinogens when he robbed the bank.

REJOINDER

relief from wrong or injury

Seeking *redress* for the injuries she had received in the accident, Doreen sued the driver of the truck that had hit her.

COALESCE

to grow together or cause to unite as one

The different factions of the organization *coalesced* to form one united front against their opponents.

REDRESS

moral uprightness

Young women used to be shipped off to finishing schools to teach them proper manners and *rectitude*.

COLLATERAL

accompanying

"Let's try to stick to the main issue here and not get into all the *collateral* questions," urged the CEO.

RECTITUDE

relating to obscure learning; known to only a few

The ideas expressed in the ancient philosophical treatise were so *recondite* that only a few scholars could appreciate them.

COLLOQUY

dialogue or conversation, conference

The congressmen held a *colloquy* to determine how to proceed with the environmental legislation.

RECONDITE

to retract a statement, opinion, etc.

The statement was so damning that the politician had no hopes of recovering his credibility, even though he tried to *recant* the words.

COLLUSION

collaboration, complicity, conspiracy

It came to light that the police chief and the mafia were in *collusion* in running the numbers racket.

RECANT

resisting authority or control

The *recalcitrant* mule refused to go down the treacherous path, however hard its master pulled at its reins.

COMELINESS

physical grace and beauty

Ann's *comeliness* made her perfect for the role of Sleeping Beauty.

RECALCITRANT

witty, skillful storyteller

The *raconteur* kept all the passengers entertained with his stories during the six-hour flight.

COMMENSURATE

proportional

Steve was given a salary *commensurate* with his experience.

RACONTEUR

occurring daily; commonplace

The sight of people singing on the street is so *quotidian* in New York that passersby rarely react to it.

COMMODIOUS

roomy, spacious

Raqiyah was able to stretch out fully in the *commodious* bathtub.

QUOTIDIAN

overly idealistic, impractical

The practical Danuta was skeptical of her roommate's *quixotic* plans to build a roller coaster in their yard.

COMPUNCTION

feeling of uneasiness caused by guilt or regret

It is often said that psychopaths have no consciences, suffering little *compunction* for the pain they cause.

QUIXOTIC

inactivity, stillness

Bears typically fall into a state of *quiescence* when they hibernate during the winter months.

CONCILIATORY

overcoming distrust or hostility

Fred made the *conciliatory* gesture of buying Abby flowers after their big fight.

QUIESCENCE

inclined to complain, irritable

Curtis's complaint letter received prompt attention after the company labeled him a *querulous* potential troublemaker.

CONGENITAL

existing since birth

The infant's *congenital* deformity was corrected through surgery.

QUERULOUS

marsh; difficult situation

Kevin realized that he needed help to get himself out of this *quagmire*.

CONGRUITY

correspondence, harmony, agreement

There was an obvious *congruity* between Mark's pleasant personality and his kind actions towards others.

QUAGMIRE

beauty

The mortals gazed in admiration at Venus, stunned by her incredible *pulchritude*.

CONJECTURE

speculation, prediction

The actor refused to comment, forcing gossip columnists to make *conjectures* on his love life.

PULCHRITUDE

quarrelsome, eager and ready to fight

The serene eighty-year-old used to be a *pugnacious* troublemaker in her youth, but she's softer now.

CONJURE

to evoke a spirit, cast a spell

The cotton candy *conjured* up the image of the fairgrounds he used to visit as a child in Arthur's mind.

PUGNACIOUS

childish, immature, silly

Olivia's boyfriend's *puerile* antics are really annoying; sometimes he acts like a five-year-old!

CONSONANT (adj.)

consistent with, in agreement with

The pitiful raise Ingrid received was *consonant* with the low opinion her manager had of her performance.

PUERILE

lustful, exhibiting lewd desires

The drunken sailor gave the buxom young waitress a *prurient* look.

CONSTRUE

to explain or interpret

> "I wasn't sure how to *construe* that last remark he made," said Delia, "but I suspect it was an insult."

PRURIENT

readily assuming different forms or characters

The *protean* Scarlet Pimpernel could play a wide variety of different characters convincingly.

CONSUMMATE (adj.)

accomplished, complete, perfect

The skater delivered a *consummate* performance, perfect in every aspect.

PROTEAN

to convert to a particular belief or religion

The Jehovah's Witnesses went from door to door in the neighborhood, *proselytizing* enthusiastically.

CONSUMMATE (v.)

to complete, fulfill

Since the marriage was never *consummated*, the couple was able to legally annul it.

PROSELYTIZE

favorable, advantageous

“I realize that I should have brought this up at a more *propitious* moment, but I don’t love you,” said the bride to the groom in the middle of their marriage vows.

CONTINENCE

self-control, self-restraint

Lucy exhibited impressive *continence* in steering clear of fattening foods, and she lost 50 pounds.

PROPITIOUS

nearness

The house's *propinquity* to the foul-smelling pig farm made it impossible to sell.

CONTRAVENE

to contradict, deny, act contrary to

The watchman *contravened* his official instructions by leaving his post for an hour.

PROPINQUITY

corrupt, degenerate

Some historians claim that it was the Romans' decadent, *profligate* behavior that led to the decline of the Roman Empire.

CONVIVIAL

sociable; fond of eating, drinking, and people

> The restaurant's *convivial* atmosphere contrasted starkly with the gloom of Maureen's empty apartment.

PROFLIGATE

vast, enormous, extraordinary

The musician's *prodigious* talent made her famous all over the world.

CONVOKE

to call together, summon

The president *convoked* a group of experts to advise him on how to deal with the crisis.

PRODIGIOUS

tendency, inclination

His *proclivity* for speeding got him into trouble with the highway patrol on many occasions.

CONVOLUTED

twisted, complicated, involved

Although many people bought *A Brief History of Time*, few could follow its *convoluted* ideas and theories.

PROCLIVITY

honesty, high-mindedness

The conscientious witness responded with the utmost *probity* to all the questions posed to her.

COPIOUS

abundant, plentiful

The hostess had prepared *copious* amounts of food for the banquet.

PROBITY

lack of usual necessities or comforts

The convict endured total *privation* while locked up in solitary confinement for a month.

CORPOREAL

having to do with the body; tangible, material

Makiko realized that the supposed ghost was *corporeal* in nature when it bumped into a chair.

PRIVATION

to lie, evade the truth

Rather than admit that he had overslept again, the employee *prevaricated*, claiming that traffic had made him late.

CORPULENCE

obesity, fatness, bulkiness

Egbert's *corpulence* increased as he spent several hours each day eating and drinking.

PREVARICATE

having foresight

Jonah's decision to sell the apartment turned out to be a *prescient* one, as its value soon dropped by half.

CORROBORATE

to confirm, verify

Fingerprints *corroborated* the witness's testimony that he saw the defendant in the victim's apartment.

PRESCIENT

preference, liking

The old woman's *predilection* for candy was evident from the chocolate bar wrappers strewn all over her apartment.

COSSET

to pamper, treat with great care

Mimi *cosseted* her toy poodle, feeding it gourmet meals and buying it a silk pillow to sleep on.

PREDILECTION

to cause to happen; to throw down from a height

It's fairly certain that Lloyd's incessant smoking *precipitated* his early death from cancer.

COUNTENANCE (n.)

facial expression; look of approval or support

Jeremy was afraid of the new Music Appreciation instructor because she had such an evil *countenance*.

PRECIPITATE (v.)

COUNTENANCE (v.)

sudden and unexpected

Since the couple wed after knowing each other only a month, many expected their *precipitate* marriage to end in divorce.

to favor, support

When the girls started a pillow fight, the baby-sitter warned them, "I will not *countenance* such behavior."

PRECIPITATE (adj.)

to speak in a pretentious manner

She *pontificated* about the virtues of being rich until we all left the room in disgust.

COUNTERMAND

to annul, cancel, make a contrary order

Protestants were relieved when the king *countermanded* his decree that they should be burned at the stake as heretics.

PONTIFICATE

controversy, argument; verbal attack

The candidate's *polemic* against his opponent was vicious and small-minded rather than well reasoned and convincing.

CRAVEN

cowardly

The *craven* lion cringed in the corner of his cage, terrified of the mouse.

POLEMIC

to use diligently; to engage; to join together

The weaver *plied* the fibers together to make a blanket.

CREDENCE

acceptance of something as true or real

Mr. Biggles couldn't give any *credence* to the charge that his darling son had cheated on his test.

PLY (v.)

to soothe or pacify

The burglar tried to *placate* the snarling Doberman by saying, “Nice doggy,” and offering it a treat.

CREDULOUS

gullible, trusting

Although some 4-year-olds believe in the Easter Bunny, only the most *credulous* 9-year-olds do.

PLACATE

meager amount or wage

Zack felt sure he would not be able to buy food for his family with the small *pittance* the government gave him.

CRESCENDO

gradual increase in volume of sound

The *crescendo* of tension became unbearable as Evel Knievel prepared to jump his motorcycle over the school buses.

PITTANCE

profound, substantial; concise, succinct, to the point

Martha's *pithy* comments during the interview must have been impressive, because she got the job.

CULPABLE

guilty, responsible for wrong

> The CEO is *culpable* for the bankruptcy of the company; he was, after all, in charge of it.

PITHY

to steal

Marianne did not *pilfer* the money for herself but rather for her sick brother, who needed medicine.

CUPIDITY

greed

The poverty-stricken man stared at the shining jewels with *cupidity* in his gleaming eyes.

PILFER

calm in temperament; sluggish

The *phlegmatic* old boar snoozed in the grass as the energetic piglets frolicked around him.

CURMUDGEON

cranky person

The old man was a notorious *curmudgeon* who snapped at anyone who disturbed him for any reason.

PHLEGMATIC

rudeness, peevishness

The child's *petulance* annoyed the teacher, who liked her young students to be cheerful and cooperative.

CURSORY

hastily done, superficial

The copy editor gave the article a *cursory* once-over, missing dozens of errors.

PETULANCE

epidemic, plague

The country went into national crisis when it was plagued by both *pestilence* and floods at the same time.

DEBASE

to degrade or lower in quality or stature

The president's deceitful actions *debased* the stature of his office.

PESTILENCE

persistent, stubborn

Despite her parents' opposition, Tina *pertinaciously* insisted on continuing to date her boyfriend.

DEBAUCH

to corrupt, seduce from virtue or duty; indulge

After the unscrupulous count *debauched* the innocent girl, she was shunned by her fellow villagers.

PERTINACIOUS

shrewd, astute, keen witted

Inspector Poirot used his *perspicacious* mind to solve mysteries.

DEBILITATE

to weaken, enfeeble

Debilitated by the flu, the postman was barely able to finish his rounds.

PERSPICACIOUS

very harmful

The Claytons considered Rocky, a convicted felon, to be a *pernicious* influence on their innocent daughter.

DEBUNK

to discredit, disprove

It was the teacher's mission in life to *debunk* the myth that girls are bad at math.

PERNICIOUS

penetrable

Karen discovered that her raincoat was *permeable* when she was drenched while wearing it in a rainstorm.

DECIDUOUS

losing leaves in the fall; short-lived, temporary

Deciduous trees are bare in winter, which is why coniferous trees such as evergreens are used as Christmas trees.

PERMEABLE

moving from place to place

Morty claims that his *peripatetic* hot dog stand gives him the opportunity to travel all over the city.

DECLIVITY

downward slope

Because the village was situated on the *declivity* of a hill, it never flooded.

PERIPATETIC

done in a routine way; indifferent

The machinelike bank teller processed the transaction and gave the waiting customer a *perfunctory* smile.

DECOROUS

proper, tasteful, socially correct

The socialite trained her daughters in the finer points of *decorous* behavior, hoping they would make a good impression at the debutante ball.

PERFUNCTORY

faithless, disloyal, untrustworthy

The actress's *perfidious* companion revealed all of her intimate secrets to the gossip columnist.

DECRY

to belittle, openly condemn

Governments all over the world *decried* the dictator's vicious massacre of the helpless peasants.

PERFIDIOUS

complete and utter loss; damnation

Faust brought *perdition* upon himself when he made a deal with the Devil in exchange for power.

DEFERENTIAL

respectful and polite in a submissive way

> The respectful young law clerk treated the Supreme Court justice very *deferentially*.

PERDITION

discerning, able to perceive

The *percipient* detective saw through the suspect's lies and uncovered the truth in the matter.

DEFT

skillful, dexterous

It was a pleasure to watch the *deft* carpenter as he repaired the furniture.

PERCIPIENT

DELETERIOUS

having bad connotations; disparaging

The teacher scolded Mark for his unduly *pejorative* comments about his classmate's presentation.

harmful, destructive, detrimental

If we put these defective clocks on the market, it could be quite *deleterious* to our reputation.

PEJORATIVE

uninspired, boring academic

The professor's tedious commentary on the subject soon gained her a reputation as a *pedant*.

DELINEATION

depiction, representation

Mrs. Baxter was very satisfied with the artist's *delineation* of her new mansion.

PEDANT

teacher

Jesus was known as an influential *pedagogue* in his society.

DELUGE

to submerge, overwhelm; flood

The popular actor was *deluged* with fan mail.

PEDAGOGUE

minor sin or offense

Gabriel tends to harp on his brother's *peccadilloes* and never lets him live them down.

DEMUR

to express doubts or objections

When scientific authorities claimed that all the planets revolved around the Earth, Galileo, with his superior understanding of the situation, was forced to *demur*.

PECCADILLO

scarcity, lack

Because of the relative *paucity* of bananas in the country, their price was very high.

DENIGRATE

to slur or blacken someone's reputation

The people still loved the president, despite his enemies' attempts to *denigrate* his character.

PAUCITY

piece of literature or music imitating other works

The playwright's clever *pastiche* of the well-known Bible story had the audience rolling in the aisles.

DEPOSE

to remove from a high position, as from a throne

After being *deposed* from his throne, the king spent the rest of his life in exile.

PASTICHE

DEPRAVITY

stinginess

Ethel gained a reputation for *parsimony* when she refused to pay for her daughter's college education.

sinfulness, moral corruption

The *depravity* of the actor's Hollywood lifestyle shocked his traditional parents.

PARSIMONY

to ward off or deflect

Kari *parried* every question the army officer fired at her, much to his frustration.

DEPRECATE

to belittle, disparage

Ernest *deprecated* his own contribution, instead praising the efforts of his coworkers.

PARRY

of limited scope or outlook, provincial

It was obvious that Victor's *parochial* mentality would clash with Ivonne's liberal open-mindedness.

DEPRECIATE

to lose value gradually

The Barrettas sold their house, fearful that its value would *depreciate* due to the nuclear reactor being built around the corner.

discussion, usually between enemies

The peace organization tried in vain to schedule a *parley* between Israel and Iraq.

DEROGATE

to belittle, disparage

The sarcastic old man never stopped *derogating* the efforts of his daughter, even after she won the Nobel Prize.

PARLEY

equality

Mrs. Lutskaya tried to maintain *parity* between her children, although each claimed she gave the other preferential treatment.

DESECRATE

to abuse something sacred

The archaeologist tried to explain to the explorer that he had *desecrated* the temple by spitting in it, but to no avail.

PARITY

impressive array

Corrina casually sifted through a *panoply* of job offers before finally deciding on one.

DESICCATE

to dry completely, dehydrate

After a few weeks of lying on the desert's baking sands, the cow's carcass became completely *desiccated*.

PANOPLY

cure-all

Some claim that vitamin C is a *panacea* for all sorts of illnesses, but I have my doubts.

DESPONDENT

feeling discouraged and dejected

Mr. Baker was lonely and *despondent* after his wife's death.

PANACEA

to make less serious, ease

The accused's crime was so vicious that the defense lawyer could not *palliate* it for the jury.

DESPOT

tyrannical ruler

The *despot* executed half the nobles in his court on a whim.

PALLIATE

to lose strength or interest

Over time, the model's beauty *palled*, though her haughty attitude remained intact.

DESTITUTE

very poor, poverty-stricken

After the stock market crash, Jeanette was *destitute*, forced to beg on the streets in order to survive.

PALL (v.)

covering that darkens or obscures; coffin

A *pall* fell over the landscape as the clouds obscured the moon in the night sky.

DESULTORY

at random, rambling, unmethodical

Diane had a *desultory* academic record; she had changed majors 12 times in three years.

PALL (n.)

DEXTEROUS

idle talk

The journalist eagerly recorded the *palaver* among the football players in the locker room.

skilled physically or mentally

The gymnast who won the contest was far more *dexterous* than the other competitors.

PALAVER

showy

The billionaire's 200-room palace was considered by many to be an overly *ostentatious* display of wealth.

DIABOLICAL

fiendish; wicked

Sherlock Holmes's archenemy is the *diabolical* Professor Moriarty.

OSTENTATIOUS

apparent

The *ostensible* reason for his visit was to borrow a book, but secretly he wanted to chat with lovely Wanda.

DIAPHANOUS

allowing light to show through; delicate

> Ginny's *diaphanous* gown failed to disguise the fact that she was wearing ripped panty hose.

OSTENSIBLE

wealth

Livingston considered his BMW to be a symbol of both *opulence* and style.

DIATRIBE

bitter verbal attack

During the CEO's lengthy *diatribe*, the board members managed to remain calm and self-controlled.

OPULENCE

burdensome

The assignment was so difficult to manage that it proved *onerous* to the team in charge of it.

DICHOTOMY

division into two parts

Westerns often feature a simple *dichotomy* between good guys and bad guys.

ONEROUS

having infinite knowledge, all-seeing

Christians believe that because God is *omniscient*, they cannot hide their sins from Him.

DICTUM

authoritative statement; popular saying

Chris tried to live his life in accordance with the *dictum* "Two wrongs don't make a right."

OMNISCIENT

too helpful, meddlesome

The *officious* waiter butted into the couple's conversation, advising them on how to take out a mortgage.

DIDACTIC

excessively instructive

The father was overly *didactic* with his children, turning every activity into a lesson.

OFFICIOUS

to shut, block

A shadow is thrown across the Earth's surface during a solar eclipse, when the light from the sun is *occluded* by the moon.

DIFFIDENCE

shyness, lack of confidence

Steve's *diffidence* during the job interview stemmed from his nervous nature and lack of experience.

OCCLUDE

to make unnecessary; to anticipate and prevent

The river was shallow enough for the riders to wade across, which *obviated* the need for a bridge.

DILATORY

slow, tending to delay

The congressman used *dilatory* measures to delay the passage of the bill.

OBVIATE

insensitive, stupid, dull, unclear

The directions were so *obtuse* that Alfred did not understand what was expected of him.

DIMINUTIVE

small

Napoleon made up for his *diminutive* stature with his aggressive personality, terrifying his courtiers.

OBTUSE

DISCONCERTING

troublesome, boisterous, unruly

The *obstreperous* toddler, who was always breaking things, was the terror of his nursery school.

bewildering, perplexing, slightly disturbing

Brad found his mother-in-law's hostile manner so *disconcerting* that he acted like a fool in her presence.

OBSTREPEROUS

overly submissive, brownnosing

The *obsequious* new employee complimented her supervisor's tie and agreed with him on every issue.

DISCURSIVE

wandering from topic to topic

The professor, known for his *discursive* speaking style, covered everything from armadillos to zebras in his zoology lecture.

OBSEQUIOUS

indirect, evasive; misleading, devious

Usually open and friendly, Allie has been behaving in a curiously *oblique* manner lately.

DISGORGE

to vomit, discharge violently

The drunken man *disgorged* huge quantities of beer, then passed out.

OBLIQUE

to make legally invalid; to counteract the effect of

Crystal *nullified* her contract with her publisher when she received a better offer from another company.

DISPARAGE

to belittle, speak disrespectfully about

Gregorio loved to *disparage* his brother's dancing skills, pointing out every mistake he made on the floor.

NULLIFY

shade of meaning

The scholars argued for hours over tiny *nuances* in the interpretation of the last line of the poem.

DISSEMBLE

to pretend, disguise one's motives

> The villain could dissemble to the police no longer—he finally had to confess to the forgery.

NUANCE

DISSEMINATE

harmful, unwholesome

The people on the sidewalk covered their noses and mouths as the bus passed to avoid breathing in the *noxious* exhaust fumes.

to spread far and wide

The wire service *disseminates* information so rapidly that events get reported shortly after they happen.

NOXIOUS

unfavorable fame

Wayne realized from the silence that greeted him as he entered the bar that his *notoriety* preceded him.

DISSENSION

difference of opinion

The government was forced to abandon the extensive reforms it had planned, due to continued *dissension* within its party ranks about the form these reforms should take.

NOTORIETY

stinking, putrid

A dead mouse trapped in your walls produces a *noisome* odor.

DISSIPATE

to scatter; to pursue pleasure to excess

The fog gradually *dissipated*, revealing all the ships docked in the harbor.

NOISOME

to irritate

I don’t particularly like having blue hair—I just do it to *nettle* my parents.

DISTEND

to swell, inflate, bloat

Her stomach was *distended* after she gorged on the six-course meal.

NETTLE (v.)

novice, beginner

A relative *neophyte* at bowling, Seth rolled all of his balls into the gutter.

DITHER

to move or act confusedly or without clear purpose

Ellen *dithered* around her apartment, uncertain how to tackle the family crisis.

NEOPHYTE

not worth considering

It's obvious from our *negligible* dropout rate that our students love our program.

DIURNAL

daily

Diurnal creatures tend to become inactive during the night.

NEGLIGIBLE

starting to develop, coming into existence

The advertising campaign was still in a *nascent* stage, and nothing had been finalized yet.

DIVINE (v.)

to foretell or know by inspiration

The fortune-teller *divined* from the pattern of the tea leaves that her customer would marry five times.

NASCENT

lowest point

As Lou waited in line to audition for the diaper commercial, he realized he had reached the *nadir* of his acting career.

DIVISIVE

creating disunity or conflict

The leader used *divisive* tactics to pit his enemies against each other.

NADIR

DOGMATIC

generous

The *munificent* millionaire donated ten million dollars to the hospital.

rigidly fixed in opinion, opinionated

The dictator was *dogmatic*—he, and only he, was right.

MUNIFICENT

diverse

Ken opened the hotel room window, letting in the *multifarious* noises of the great city.

DOLEFUL

sad, mournful

Looking into the *doleful* eyes of the lonely pony, the girl decided to take him home with her.

MULTIFARIOUS

DROLL

to mark with spots

Food stains *mottled* the tablecloth.

amusing in a wry, subtle way

Although the play couldn't be described as hilarious, it was certainly *droll*.

MOTTLE

dying, decaying

Thanks to the feminist movement, many sexist customs are now *moribund* in this society.

DULCET

pleasant sounding, soothing to the ear

The *dulcet* tone of her voice lulled me to sleep.

MORIBUND

frivolity, gaiety, laughter

Vera's hilarious jokes contributed to the general *mirth* at the dinner party.

DURESS

threat of force or intimidation; imprisonment

Under *duress*, the political dissident revealed the names of others in her organization to the secret police.

MIRTH

to operate against, work against

Lenin *militated* against the tsar for years before he overthrew him and established the Soviet Union.

DYSPEPTIC

suffering from indigestion; gloomy and irritable

The *dyspeptic* young man cast a gloom over the party the minute he walked in.

MILITATE

courageousness; endurance

The helicopter pilot showed her *mettle* as she landed in the battlefield to rescue the wounded soldiers.

EBB

to fade away, recede

Melissa enjoyed watching the *ebb* and flow of the tide from her beachside balcony.

METTLE

extremely careful, fastidious, painstaking

To find all the clues at the crime scene, the investigators *meticulously* examined every inch of the area.

EBULLIENT

exhilarated, full of enthusiasm and high spirits

The *ebullient* child exhausted the baby-sitter, who lacked the energy to keep up with her.

METICULOUS

quick, shrewd, and unpredictable

Her *mercurial* personality made it difficult to guess how she would react to the bad news.

EDICT

law, command, official public order

Pedestrians often disobey the *edict* that they should not jaywalk.

MERCURIAL

EDIFY

beggar

"Please, sir, can you spare a dime?" begged the *mendicant* as the businessman walked past.

to instruct morally and spiritually

The guru was paid to *edify* the actress in the ways of Buddhism.

MENDICANT

dishonest

So many of her stories were *mendacious* that I decided she must be a pathological liar.

EFFACE

to erase or make illegible

Benjamin attempted to *efface* all traces of his troubled past by assuming a completely new identity.

MENDACIOUS

overly sentimental

The mother's death should have been a touching scene, but the movie's treatment of it was so *maudlin* that, instead of making the audience cry, it made them cringe.

EFFICACIOUS

effective, efficient

Penicillin was one of the most *efficacious* drugs on the market when it was first introduced; the drug completely eliminated almost all bacterial infections for which it was administered.

MAUDLIN

to enroll as a member of a college or university

When Suda-May *matriculates* at Yale University this coming fall, she'll move to New Haven.

EFFIGY

stuffed doll; likeness of a person

The anti-American militants burned Uncle Sam in *effigy* during their demonstration.

MATRICULATE

strict disciplinarian, one who rigidly follows rules

A complete *martinet*, the official insisted that Pete fill out all the forms again even though he was already familiar with his case.

EFFRONTERY

impudent boldness; audacity

The receptionist had the *effrontery* to laugh out loud when the CEO tripped over a computer wire and fell flat on his face.

MARTINET

to evade responsibility by pretending to be ill

A common way to dodge the draft was by *malingering*—faking an illness so as to avoid having to serve in the Army.

EFFULGENT

brilliantly shining

The *effulgent* stars that filled the dark evening sky dazzled the sharecroppers.

MALINGER

clumsy, tactless

“So, when is your baby due?” said the *maladroit* guest to his overweight but not pregnant hostess.

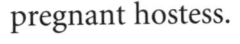

EFFUSIVE

expressing emotion without restraint

The teacher praised Brian *effusively* for his brilliant essay.

MALADROIT

generous, noble in spirit

Although at first he seemed mean, Uncle Frank turned out to be a very *magnanimous* fellow.

EGREGIOUS

conspicuously bad

The English textbook contained several *egregious* errors; for example, "grammar" was misspelled as "gramer" throughout.

MAGNANIMOUS

whirlpool; turmoil; agitated state of mind

The transportation system of the city had collapsed in the *maelstrom* of war.

EGRESS

exit

Airplanes should have points of convenient *egress* so that passengers can escape in the event of a crash.

MAELSTROM

plot or scheme

Tired of his enemies' endless *machinations* to remove him from the throne, the king had them executed.

ELUCIDATE

to explain, clarify

The teacher *elucidated* the reasons why she had failed the student to his upset parents.

MACHINATION

sorrowful, mournful; dismal

Irish wakes are a rousing departure from the *lugubrious* funeral services most people are accustomed to.

ENDEMIC

belonging to a particular area, inherent

The health department determined that the outbreak was *endemic* to the small village, so they quarantined the inhabitants before the virus could spread.

LUGUBRIOUS

easily flexed, limber, agile

The *lissome* yoga instructor twisted herself into shapes that her students could only dream of.

ENERVATE

to weaken, sap strength from

The guerrillas hoped that a series of surprise attacks would *enervate* the regular army.

LISSOME

to treat as a celebrity

After the success of his novel, the author was *lionized* by the press.

ENGENDER

to produce, cause, bring about

> His fear of clowns was *engendered* when he witnessed the death of his father at the hands of a clown.

LIONIZE

clear, transparent

Shelley could see all the way to the bottom through the pond's *limpid* water.

ENMITY

hostility, antagonism, ill will

After Adams was killed by Bell, the *enmity* between their families continued for hundreds of years.

LIMPID

trickery

The magician was skilled in the arts of *legerdemain*.

ENNUI

boredom, lack of interest and energy

Joe tried to alleviate the *ennui* he felt while doing his tedious job by flirting with all his coworkers.

LEGERDEMAIN

lethargy, sluggishness

The defeated French army plunged into a state of depressed *lassitude* as they trudged home from Russia.

ENSCONCE

to settle comfortably into a place

Wayne sold the big, old family house and *ensconced* his aged mother in a cozy little cottage.

LASSITUDE

dawdler, loafer, lazy person

The manager hesitated to fire Biff, his incompetent *laggard* of an assistant, because Biff was the CEO's son.

ENTREAT

to plead, beg

I *entreated* him to just tell me what the problem was instead of bottling it up inside, but he refused.

LAGGARD

using few words

She was a *laconic* poet who built her reputation on using words as sparingly as possible.

EPHEMERAL

momentary, transient, fleeting

The lives of mayflies seem *ephemeral* to us, since the flies' average life span is a matter of hours.

LACONIC

tearful

Heather always became *lachrymose* when it was time to bid her daughter good-bye.

EPICURE

person with refined taste in food and wine

Restaurant critics should be *epicures*, as people rely on their judgments in choosing where to eat.

LACHRYMOSE

sound of a funeral bell; omen of death or failure

When the townspeople heard the *knelling* from the church belfry, they knew that their mayor had died.

EPIGRAM

short, witty saying or poem

The poet was renowned for his skill in making up amusing *epigrams*.

KNELL

side-by-side placement

The porcelain dog was placed in *juxtaposition* with the straw doghouse on the mantelpiece.

EQUANIMITY

calmness, composure

Kelly took the news that she had been fired with outward *equanimity*, though she was crying inside.

JUXTAPOSITION

philosophy of law

An expert in *jurisprudence*, the esteemed lawyer was often consulted by his colleagues.

ERUDITE

learned, scholarly

The annual meeting of professors brought together the most *erudite*, respected individuals in the field.

JURISPRUDENCE

huge force destroying everything in its path

The *juggernaut* of Napoleon's army surged ahead until it was halted in its tracks by the brutal winter.

ESOTERIC

understood by only a learned few

Only a handful of experts are knowledgeable about the *esoteric* world of particle physics.

JUGGERNAUT

belligerent support of one's country

The president's *jingoism* made him declare war on other countries at the slightest provocation.

ETHEREAL

not earthly, spiritual, delicate

Her delicate, *ethereal* beauty made her a popular model for pre-Raphaelite artists.

JINGOISM

envious; obnoxious

It is cruel and *invidious* for parents to play favorites with their children.

ETHOS

beliefs or character of a group

In accordance with the *ethos* of his people, the teenage boy underwent a series of initiation rituals to become a man.

INVIDIOUS

verbal abuse

A stream of *invective* poured from Mrs. Pratt's mouth as she watched the vandals smash her ceramic frog.

EVANESCENT

momentary, transitory, short-lived

It is lucky that eclipses are *evanescent*, or the world would never see sunlight.

INVECTIVE

to harden; accustom; become used to

Eventually, Hassad became *inured* to the sirens that went off every night and could sleep through them.

EVINCE

to show clearly, display, signify

The new secretary *evinced* impressive typing and filing skills.

INURE

uncompromising, refusing to be reconciled

The professor was *intransigent* on the deadline, insisting that everyone turn the assignment in on Friday.

EXACERBATE

to aggravate, intensify the bad qualities of

It is unwise to take aspirin to relieve heartburn; instead of providing relief, the drug will only *exacerbate* the problem.

INTRANSIGENT

to insert; to intervene

The policeman *interposed* himself between the two men who were about to start fighting.

EXCULPATE

to clear of blame or fault, vindicate

The adversarial legal system is intended to convict those who are guilty and to *exculpate* those who are innocent.

INTERPOSE

to insert; change by adding new words or material

The editor *interpolated* a few new sentences into the manuscript, and the new edition was ready to print.

EXECRABLE

utterly detestable, abhorrent

The stew tasted *execrable* after the cook accidentally dumped a pound of salt into it.

INTERPOLATE

trespasser; meddler in others' affairs

The wolf pack rejected the lone pup as an *interloper*.

EXHORT

to urge or incite by strong appeals

Rob's friends *exhorted* him to beware of ice on the roads when he insisted on driving home in the middle of a snowstorm.

INTERLOPER

to forbid, prohibit

The matron *interdicted* male visits to the girls' dorm rooms after midnight.

EXHUME

to remove from a grave; uncover a secret

The murder victim's corpse was *exhumed*, but no new evidence was discovered and it was reburied the following day.

INTERDICT

sly, treacherous, devious

Iago's *insidious* comments about Desdemona fuelled Othello's feelings of jealousy regarding his wife.

EXIGENT

urgent; excessively demanding

The patient was losing blood so rapidly that it was *exigent* to stop the source of the bleeding.

INSIDIOUS

sin, evil act

"I promise to close every den of *iniquity* in this town!" thundered the conservative new mayor.

EXONERATE

to clear of blame, absolve

The fugitive was *exonerated* when another criminal confessed to committing the crime.

INIQUITY

hostile, unfriendly

Even though a cease-fire had been in place for months, the two sides were still *inimical* to each other.

EXPEDIENT (adj.)

convenient, efficient, practical

It was considered more *expedient* to send the fruit directly to the retailer instead of through a middleman.

INIMICAL

entrance

Ed hoped that the mailroom job would provide him with an *ingress* into the company.

EXPIATE

to atone for, make amends for

The nun *expiated* her sins by scrubbing the floor of the convent on her hands and knees.

INGRESS

straightforward, open; naive and unsophisticated

She was so *ingenuous* that her friends feared that her innocence would be exploited when she visited the big city.

EXPURGATE

to censor

Government propagandists *expurgated* all negative references to the dictator from the film.

INGENUOUS

EXTEMPORANEOUS

original, clever, inventive

Luther found an *ingenious* way to solve the complex math problem.

unrehearsed, on the spur of the moment

Jan gave an *extemporaneous* performance of a Monty Python skit at her surprise birthday party.

INGENIOUS

inflexible, unyielding

The *inexorable* force of the twister swept away their house.

EXTRICATE

to free from, disentangle

The fly was unable to *extricate* itself from the flypaper.

INEXORABLE

unable to move, tending to inactivity

In the heat of the desert afternoon, lizards lie *inert*.

FALLOW

uncultivated, unused

This field should lie *fallow* for a year so that the soil does not become completely depleted.

INERT

unquestionable

His *indubitable* cooking skills made it all the more astonishing when the Thanksgiving dinner he prepared tasted awful.

FASTIDIOUS

careful with details

Brett was normally so *fastidious* that Rachel was astonished to find his desk littered with clutter.

INDUBITABLE

habitually lazy, idle

Her *indolent* ways got her fired from many jobs.

FATUOUS

stupid; foolishly self-satisfied

Ted's *fatuous* comments always embarrassed his keen-witted wife at parties.

INDOLENT

angry, incensed, offended

The innocent passerby was *indignant* when the police treated him as a suspect in the crime.

FECUND

fertile, fruitful, productive

The *fecund* housewife gave birth to a total of twenty children.

INDIGNANT

FELICITOUS

very poor

Because the suspect was *indigent*, the state paid for his legal representation.

suitable, appropriate; well spoken

The father of bride made a *felicitous* speech at the wedding, contributing to the success of the event.

INDIGENT

never tired

Theresa seemed *indefatigable*, barely sweating after a 10-mile run.

FERVID

passionate, intense, zealous

The fans of Maria Callas were particularly *fervid*, doing anything to catch a glimpse of the great singer.

INDEFATIGABLE

sudden invasion

The army was unable to resist the *incursion* of the rebel forces into their territory.

FETID

foul-smelling, putrid

The *fetid* stench from the outhouse caused Laura to wrinkle her nose in disgust.

INCURSION

to blame, charge with a crime

His suspicious behavior after the break-in led authorities to *inculpate* him.

FETTER

to bind, chain, confine

The chain gang, *fettered* together in a long line, trudged slowly through the mud.

INCULPATE

to teach, impress in the mind

Most parents blithely *inculcate* their children with their religious beliefs instead of allowing their children to select their own faith.

FLACCID

limp, flabby, weak

The woman jiggled her *flaccid* arms in disgust, resolving to begin lifting weights as soon as possible.

INCULCATE

beginning to exist or appear; in an initial stage

At that point, her cancer was only *incipient* and she could still work full time.

FLORID

gaudy, extremely ornate; ruddy, flushed

> The palace had been decorated in an excessively *florid* style; every surface had been carved and gilded.

INCIPIENT

imperfectly formed or formulated

As her thoughts on the subject were still in *inchoate* form, Amy could not explain what she meant.

FOIBLE

minor weakness or character flaw

Her habit of licking out the centers of Oreo cookies is just a *foible*, although it is somewhat annoying.

INCHOATE

combustible, flammable, burning easily

Gasoline is so *incendiary* that cigarette smoking is forbidden at gas stations.

FOMENT

to arouse or incite

> The protesters tried to *foment* feeling against the war through their speeches and demonstrations.

to call into question, attack verbally

"How dare you *impugn* my honorable motives?" protested the lawyer on being accused of ambulance chasing.

FORBEARANCE

patience, restraint, leniency

In light of the fact that he was new on the job, Collette decided to exercise *forbearance* with her assistant's numerous errors.

IMPUGN

without planning or foresight, negligent

The *improvident* woman spent all the money she received in her court settlement within two weeks.

FORSWEAR

to repudiate, renounce, disclaim, reject

I was forced to *forswear* French fries after the doctor told me that my cholesterol was too high.

IMPROVIDENT

FORTE

to ask repeatedly, beg

The assistant *importuned* her boss with constant requests for a raise and promotion.

strong point, something a person does well

Since math was Dan's *forte*, his friends always asked him to calculate the bill whenever they went out to dinner together.

IMPORTUNE

quick to act without thinking

The *impetuous* day trader rushed to sell his stocks at the first hint of trouble, and lost $300,000.

FOUNDER (v.)

to fall helplessly; sink

After colliding with the jagged rock, the ship *foundered*, forcing the crew to abandon it.

IMPETUOUS

impossible to penetrate; incapable of being affected

A good raincoat should be *impervious* to moisture.

FRACAS

noisy dispute

When the bandits discovered that the gambler was cheating them at cards, a violent *fracas* ensued.

IMPERVIOUS

poor, having no money

After the crash of thousands of tech startups, many Internet millionaires found themselves *impecunious*.

FRACTIOUS

unruly, rebellious

The general had a hard time maintaining discipline among his *fractious* troops.

IMPECUNIOUS

unchangeable, invariable

Poverty was an *immutable* fact of life for the unfortunate Wood family; every moneymaking scheme they tried failed.

FULSOME

sickeningly excessive; repulsive

Diana felt nauseous at the sight of the rich, *fulsome* dishes weighing down the table at the banquet.

IMMUTABLE

to infuse; dye, wet, moisten

Marcia struggled to *imbue* her children with decent values, a difficult task in this day and age.

GAMBOL

to dance or skip around playfully

The parents gathered to watch the children *gambol* about the yard.

IMBUE

type or kind

“I try not to associate with men of his *ilk*,” sniffed the respectable old lady.

GARNER

to gather and store

> The director managed to *garner* financial backing from several different sources for her next project.

ILK

GARRULOUS

disgraceful and dishonorable

He was humiliated by his *ignominious* dismissal.

very talkative

The *garrulous* parakeet distracted its owner with its continuous talking.

IGNOMINIOUS

peculiarity of temperament, eccentricity

His numerous *idiosyncrasies* included a fondness for wearing bright green shoes with mauve socks.

GIBE

to make heckling, taunting remarks

Tina *gibed* at her brothers mercilessly as they clumsily attempted to pitch the tent.

IDIOSYNCRASY

one who attacks traditional beliefs

His lack of regard for traditional beliefs soon established him as an *iconoclast*.

GLIB

fluent in an insincere manner; offhand, casual

The slimy politician managed to continue gaining supporters because he was a *glib* speaker.

ICONOCLAST

purposeful exaggeration for effect

When the mayor claimed his town was one of the seven wonders of the world, outsiders classified his statement as *hyperbole.*

GNOSTIC

having to do with knowledge

The *gnostics* were distrusted by the Church because of their preference for knowledge over faith.

HYPERBOLE

very old; whitish or gray from age

> The old man's *hoary* beard contrasted starkly to the new stubble of his teenage grandson.

GOAD

to prod or urge

Denise *goaded* her sister Leigh into running the marathon with her.

HOARY

wilderness

The anthropologists noticed that the people had moved out of the cities and into the *hinterland*.

GRATIS

free, costing nothing

The college students swarmed around the *gratis* buffet in the lobby.

HINTERLAND

excessively rigid; dry and stiff

The *hidebound* old patriarch would not tolerate any opposition to his orders.

GUILE

trickery, deception

Greg used considerable *guile* to acquire his rent-controlled apartment, even claiming to be a Vietnam Vet.

HIDEBOUND

tightly sealed

The *hermetic* seal of the jar proved impossible to break.

GUSTATORY

relating to sense of taste

> Murdock claimed that he loved cooking because he enjoyed the *gustatory* pleasures in life.

HERMETIC

extremely distressing, terrifying

We stayed up all night listening to Dave and Will talk about their *harrowing* adventures at sea.

HACKNEYED

worn out by overuse

We always mock my father for his *hackneyed* expressions and dated hairstyle.

HARROWING

precursor, sign of something to come

The groundhog's appearance on February 2 is a *harbinger* of spring.

HAPLESS

unfortunate, having bad luck

I wish someone would give that poor, *hapless* soul some food and shelter.

HARBINGER

SAT ROOT LIST

A, AN—not, without

AB, A—from, away, apart

AC, ACR—sharp, sour

AD, A—to, towards

ALI, ALTR—another

AM, AMI—love

AMBI, AMPHI—both

AMBL, AMBUL—walk

ANIM—mind, spirit, breath

ANN, ENN—year

ANTE, ANT—before

ANTHROP—human

ANTI, ANT—against, opposite

AUD—hear

AUTO—self

BELLI, BELL—war

BENE, BEN—good

BI—two

BIBLIO—book

BIO—life

BURS—money, purse

CAD, CAS, CID—happen, fall

CAP, CIP—head

CARN—flesh

CAP, CAPT, CEPT, CIP—take, hold, seize

CED, CESS—yield, go

CHROM—color

CHRON—time

CIDE—murder

CIRCUM—around

CLIN, CLIV—slope

CLUD, CLUS, CLAUS, CLOIS—shut, close

CO, COM, CON—with, together

COGN, GNO—know

CONTRA—against

CORP—body

COSMO, COSM—world

CRAC, CRAT—rule, power

CRED—trust, believe

CRESC, CRET—grow

CULP—blame, fault

CURR, CURS—run

DE—down, out, apart

DEC—ten, tenth

DEMO, DEM—people

DI, DIURN—day

DIA—across

DIC, DICT—speak

DIS, DIF, DI—not, apart, away

DOC, DOCT—teach

DOL—pain

DUC, DUCT—lead

EGO—self

EN, EM—in, into

ERR—wander

EU—well, good

EX, E—out, out of

FAC, FIC, FECT, FY, FEA—make, do

FAL, FALS—deceive

FERV—boil

FID—faith, trust

FLU, FLUX—flow

FORE—before

FRAG, FRAC—break

FUS—pour

GEN—birth, class, kin

GRAD, GRESS—step

GRAPH, GRAM—writing

GRAT—pleasing

GRAV, GRIEV—heavy

GREG—crowd, flock

HABIT, HIBIT—have, hold

HAP—by chance

HELIO, HELI—sun

HETERO—other

HOL—whole

HOMO—same

HOMO—man

HYDR—water

HYPER—too much, excess

HYPO—too little, under

IN, IG, IL, IM, IR—not

IN, IL, IM, IR—in, on, into

INTER—between, among

INTRA, INTR—within

IT, ITER—between, among

JECT, JET—throw

JOUR—day

JUD—judge

JUNCT, JUG—join

JUR—swear, law

LAT—side

LAV, LAU, LU—wash

LEG, LEC, LEX—read, speak

LEV—light

LIBER—free

LIG, LECT—choose, gather

LIG, LI, LY—bind

LING, LANG—tongue

LITER—letter

LITH—stone

LOQU, LOC, LOG—speech, thought

LUC, LUM—light

LUD, LUS—play

MACRO—great

MAG, MAJ, MAS, MAX—great

MAL—bad

MAN—hand

MAR—sea

MATER, MATR—mother

MEDI—middle

MEGA—great

MEM, MEN—remember

METER, METR, MENS—measure

MICRO—small

MIS—wrong, bad, hate

MIT, MISS—send

MOLL—soft

MON, MONIT—warn

MONO—one

MOR—custom, manner

MOR, MORT—dead

MORPH—shape

MOV, MOT, MOB, MOM—move

MUT—change

NAT, NASC—born

NAU, NAV—ship, sailor

NEG—not, deny

NEO—new

NIHIL—none, nothing

NOM, NYM—name

NOX, NIC, NEC, NOC—harm

NOV—new

NUMER—number

OB—against

OMNI—all

ONER—burden

OPER—work

PAC—peace

PALP—feel

PAN—all

PATER, PATR—father

PATH, PASS—feel, suffer

PEC—money

PED, POD—foot

PEL, PULS—drive

PEN—almost

PEND, PENS—hang

PER—through, by, for, throughout

PER—against, destruction

PERI—around

PET—seek, go towards

PHIL—love

PHOB—fear

PHON—sound

PLAC—calm, please

PON, POS—put, place

PORT—carry

POT—drink

POT—power

PRE—before

PRIM, PRI—first

PRO—ahead, forth

PROTO—first

PROX, PROP—near

PSEUDO—false

PYR—fire

QUAD, QUAR, QUAT—four

QUES, QUER, QUIS, QUIR—question

QUIE—quiet

QUINT, QUIN—five

RADI, RAMI—branch

RECT, REG—straight, rule

REG—king, rule

RETRO—backward

RID, RIS—laugh

ROG—ask

RUD—rough, crude

RUPT—break

SACR, SANCT—holy

SCRIB, SCRIPT, SCRIV—write

SE—apart, away

SEC, SECT, SEG—cut

SED, SID—sit

SEM—seed, sow

SEN—old

SENT, SENS—feel, think

SEQU, SECU—follow

SIM, SEM—similar, same

SIGN—mark, sign

SIN—curve

SOL—sun

SOL—alone

SOMN—sleep

SON—sound

SOPH—wisdom

SPEC, SPIC—see, look

SPER—hope

SPERS, SPAR—scatter

SPIR—breathe

STRICT, STRING—bind

STRUCT, STRU—build

SUB—under

SUMM—highest

SUPER, SUR—above

SURGE, SURRECT—rise

SYN, SYM—together

TACIT, TIC—silent

TACT, TAG, TANG—touch

TEN, TIN, TAIN—hold, twist

TEND, TENS, TENT—stretch

TERM—end

TERR—earth, land

TEST—witness

THE—god

THERM—heat

TIM—fear, frightened

TOP—place

TORT—twist

TORP—stiff, numb

TOX—poison

TRACT—draw

TRANS—across, over, through, beyond

TREM, TREP—shake

TURB—shake

UMBR—shadow

UNI, UN—one

URB—city

VAC—empty

VAL, VAIL—value, strength

VEN, VENT—come

VER—true

VERB—word

VERT, VERS—turn

VICT, VINC—conquer

VID, VIS—see

VIL—base, mean

VIV, VIT—life

VOC, VOK, VOW—call, voice

VOL—wish

VOLV, VOLUT—turn, roll

VOR—eat